Happiness in Your Life - Book Four: Trust

Doe Zantamata

Copyright © 2020 Iko Productions, Inc.

All rights reserved.

ISBN: 9798673944189

Independently Published

DEDICATION

For Joy and Dean

CONTENTS

	Acknowledgments	i
1	The Importance of Trust	1
2	Trust in Yourself	11
3	Formation of Trust: Childhood	27
4	Trust in Other People	33
5	Trust and Connection	45
6	How to Build and Maintain Trust	63
7	All About Lying	79
8	Breaking Trust with Good Intentions	109
9	Trust in the World, Universal Laws, and God	123

Legal Disclaimer:

This book does not provide medical advice.

The information, including but not limited to, text, graphics, images and other material contained in this book are for informational purposes only. The purpose of this book is to promote broad consumer understanding and knowledge of various health topics. It is not intended to be a substitute for professional medical advice, diagnosis or treatment. Always seek the advice of your physician or other qualified health care provider with any questions you may have regarding a medical condition or treatment and before undertaking a new health care regimen, and never disregard professional medical advice or delay in seeking it because of something you have read in this book.

ACKNOWLEDGMENTS

Thank you to all those who have been with me on this journey, even if just for a little while.
Thank you to you who is reading this book for our connection within these pages and beyond.

1 THE IMPORTANCE OF TRUST

The importance of trust in life and relationships cannot be understated. It is the most valuable quality for peace of mind in everyday life.

Most people don't even realize just how much we all trust total strangers in the world. Every day, you go out in your car and trust that the other people in their cars will follow the rules about white, painted lines dividing lanes, red lights meaning they are going to stop, and a general respect for safety of themselves as well as others. Seeing a person run through a red light or cut you off is a jarring experience, met with shock and often anger. *They are not supposed to do that! They could cause an accident! They almost hurt me!* But then we soon go back to trusting everyone, with awareness and caution always, but we don't assume everyone will be like that wayward driver. This means we don't have to be paranoid at every red light. It means we don't have to have our heart race every time we step into the car, believing there's a strong possibility that we are going to crash. If we actually do have an accident, especially a bad one, this trust can be temporarily shattered as the trauma of the pain is very fresh. But with time and more practice, we get used to the driving experience as a positive and necessary one again.

Now, think about the way we view trust in personal relationships and how we act, who we blame, and what we decide to do after a bad experience. If a person runs a red light and causes an accident, we do not blame ourselves for being there or for not seeing things that couldn't be seen ~ their intentions or motivations for breaking that trust. Those were in *their* mind, not ours. But if a partner is being deceptive; having an affair or hiding financial information, we so often blame the victim for not seeing things they couldn't have seen. And with that blame comes a motivation to "correct" the situation for the future by shutting off trust completely, which actually makes life much worse for everyone. Living in a world without trust is truly painful.

When a person says, "trust is something that needs to be earned," it's a big sign that this person's trust was broken one too many times, and they got fed up. See, often when someone has been blindsided by a pathological liar or taken by a con, they feel hurt and stupid and vow to never trust anyone ever again. They will slam shut the castle door, and say things like, "I've been burned before, never again!"

Well that's not fair.

Do they expect they're the only ones who have ever been hurt in this world and that they will also have to compete in the Trust Olympics with any new person they meet?

Even in our own justice system, regardless of how many people may or may not be guilty of an actual crime that has already occurred, we go by "innocent until proven guilty beyond a reasonable doubt."

But people who go by the *trust has to be earned* philosophy are already convicting every single person in the world for crimes that don't even exist and think that's a good way to go. It's not. No honest, good person with a healthy self-esteem will sign up for this. Why would they? Even if they like someone, being convicted and jailed mentally and emotionally is unfair punishment and it's hurtful to someone who has done nothing wrong.

So the only people then who would go along with it are people with really low self-esteem who will resent the treatment later, or people who think lying is a fun game and will play to win, thereby ruining the person's trust even more. Having this philosophy would actually make a person more prone to attracting that which they can't stand and were trying to avoid.

Without trust, stories are invented, and drama flows freely. With trust, a person can take people's word at face value, not read into things negatively, and just be happier. It was not up to you to be lied to, but it is up to you to trust again. Absolutely if a relationship has just broken down due to abuse of trust, a trauma has occurred. A victim can't be expected to just pretend like everything is OK. They will need time to process and heal those wounds and rebuild their own sense of trust. But that shouldn't be a lifetime sentence for the victim. All that would do is create in them a paranoid driver of life who thinks every person is going to cross over all the lines and run all the red lights. What a terrible way to live. And unfair to all those people who were and were going to continue to be good and trustworthy individuals. They don't deserve to be questioned or investigated with a skeptical eye for what someone else did. If they don't know what's really happening, then they will become a victim in a different way. All that interrogating will cause them to doubt and question themselves and make them feel as though they have to walk on eggshells all the time. They deserve better treatment than that.

Not trusting anyone's motives when they give gifts can also be very hurtful. Yes, some people only give because they want to have some kind of control or deceitful motive, or strings attached. But if someone genuinely gives you something, something that took them time to make and or money and consideration and you have that mistrust for all people, you may absolutely ruin what could be a beautiful experience. You may be skeptical and say, "What, are you trying to get rid of it?" or, "What's this for? Do you need something?"

You can't redo memories.

Once a moment of kindness is met with reactions such as these, it's ruined. The person who extended kindness to you was hurt. Their effort and consideration towards you becomes a moment of regret because it was met with mistrust. Apologies or, "what, I was just asking" won't fix it. And you are teaching them not to extend kindness to you in the future unless they'd like to be hurt again. Trust is as necessary to a happy, healthy relationship as air is to the lungs. With it, a relationship can survive almost anything. Without it, almost nothing.

So first thing's first. Can we please stop blaming the wrong people when it comes to broken trust and manipulation? Can we please stop complimenting the ones who are to blame? How many times have you heard, he or she is a "good liar?" Or that a spouse who has been cheated on was "stupid" for not knowing or seeing any signs. We are blaming the person who was honest and trusted and complimenting the person who ruined the whole thing. How about instead of calling a person a "good liar" we say that they are terrible at telling the truth? Or how about instead of saying someone is a skillful or brilliant manipulator, we say they believe they have nothing to offer so they have to try and fool people into being around them instead of actually working on themselves to become a better person that people actually want to be around. Or a con artist. Artist? Really? Can't even earn a decent honest living so they put time and effort into deceiving people and always knowing that any day it could all come crashing down? What's smart about that? Where's the art or skill? It's really a waste of their time as well as the time of other people, and really, ultimately ~ a waste of life. There's nothing smart, clever, skillful, or admirable about that. And it's certainly not an "art." To those people...The art of wasting your life and anyone else whose life you happen to touch isn't impressive. It doesn't make you smarter than anyone, that's for sure. To spend this one precious life of yours living a lie. What a waste.

You are not a fool for trusting someone who lied to you. They are the fool for lying to someone who trusted them. It's the easiest thing in the world to get away with temporarily, and the hardest thing to recover from permanently. Please don't let it change you. There are already way too many of them and far too few of you.

Trust has several distinct levels.
1) Trust in yourself
2) Trust in other people, including individuals, close relationships, acquaintances, and strangers, as well as groups or institutions; government, corporations, and cultures
3) Trust in the World, a Higher Power or Order–spiritual or non-spiritual laws or entities

In general, people have more trust on a one on one level than they do of groups, especially groups that they feel are very different or more powerful than themselves. While it's true, a speaker or politician can connect with many people in a crowded room or even a country, it's a different and less intimate connection than the one that exists between two individuals. One on one is the deepest connection possible outside of one's own self. Paradoxically, the connection you have with yourself largely determines the connection or trust that you are able to feel for the world. That may not seem to make sense, but it's all about the mirror. What you believe exists is what you will gravitate towards and how you will assemble bits of information to connect the dots on how the story will make sense in your mind.

Two people can view the exact same thing but see it entirely differently. Perception and processing occur entirely in one's own mind.

2 TRUST IN YOURSELF

Trust in yourself has a variety of different sources and strengths as well as weaknesses. Weaknesses are opportunities to grow. But to grow, you need to be honest with yourself about them. You need to take responsibility for your part in their recreation in your life. Once you do this, without shame, you confront them. Once you confront them, they lose their power to control you. Change isn't instant, nor often easy, but it is possible with effort over time. Journaling can help sort your thoughts out and get them into a more concrete form that you can evaluate and look back on to see your progress. Trust in yourself goes hand in hand with confidence in yourself. The more you trust and have confidence in yourself, the less vulnerable you will be in all of those areas. For example, if you don't trust your own judgment, you may defer to the judgment of others when it comes to decisions about your life. You may believe they know what's best for you because you don't trust yourself enough. You know yourself more than any other person.

When you become aware of your motivations; fears, drives, and loves, you will become more conscious of yourself and your life and the dynamics of your closest relationships. When you examine your motivations, make sure they are not out of fear, insecurity, or trying to run away from or avoid unhappiness, chaos, change, or any conflict whatsoever. Make sure your motivations are out of love, trust, and move within and flow towards happiness and peace. If you find your motivations were of the first sort and begin to correct them, you will become more self-reliant, confident, peaceful, and less dependent on others. That doesn't mean you won't have anyone around, but it does likely mean you'll develop a different circle, or the dynamics within your current circle will change for the better. You'll attract and be attracted less to controlling people, and you'll feel more comfortable around people who have no interest in telling you what you should do or how to live your life. Change can seem scary and new territory always involves uncertainty, but if you can get used to the awkwardness, your first wobbly steps will turn into the dance of your life.

Those who wish to control other people may lose interest in you and go find other people to control. Or they may also see the strain on relationships that the control dynamic creates and choose to grow with you. Either way, the problem will be solved.

If you think of the different ways you either trust or don't trust yourself, you can begin to get a gauge on your starting point. You can feel really good about the areas you're naturally good in, and the ones you've worked to develop. You can also identify those areas where your focus and attention on improvement will be.

Ask yourself how much you trust yourself with:

1. **Money** – money is representative of value. If you don't trust yourself with money, it could be because you don't believe you have value, you don't believe your work has value, you are holding on to old beliefs that you are irresponsible and must hand over decisions about money to someone who you perceive as more responsible than you, or you reject it because you associate it with arguments. Those are just a few of the reasons. You may have your own in addition to or instead of any of these.

2. **Abilities** – How good of an anything are you? In your opinion. How good of a person? How good of a friend? How good of a mother, father, sibling, or spouse? How good are you at the work you do? Are you more afraid of being overconfident than underconfident in your abilities? If you are underconfident in your abilities, then you're actually not being humble, but acting on fear of not being

enough. Beliefs come true, so acting on that fear will make you more likely to see it realized in reality and reflected back to you. Overconfident isn't a bed of roses either, but if you look back in your life and see patterns of not believing in yourself enough, you can probably guess that's your automatic response. Confidence in your abilities means being able to discern where your intelligence, work, effort, and time have made a positive difference and had great results. To push away compliments for effort and skill means to reject positive feedback which is an essential affirmation loop. Inner-outer, outer-inner. If you reject all good words about let's say your work skills, and then you start working for someone who trashes your ability… You'll have no backup proof to yourself that what this person is saying isn't true even though it may actually be their true opinion. If you do that, you'll be more likely to try and bend and mold to what you think they want instead of recognizing that if you're good and doing your best and they are horrified with that, this isn't the place for you. You'd both be better served with others who are more in alignment.

3. **Judgment of Character** – It may be that you falsely believe that to only see the positive in people is a great way to be. When you first meet someone, you'll be more likely to dismiss your intuition that they are not of good character as something innocent. *They must be nervous. They were probably tired. I may have been too upfront.* You may also deny your own eyes or make up excuses or downplay outright lies or shady behavior that you see them say and do because you want to like them, and you couldn't really like them if you acknowledged those things you're seeing and hearing. When you have an uneasy feeling about someone, try to stay unbiased and continue to observe. Don't assign innocent theories to every awkward feeling you have, or you will end up going down repeated pathways where you gradually lose yourself until a big wake-up call has you looking to the past at all of those red flags you tossed aside with good intentions.

Judgment of character can work the opposite way,

too. If you have been hurt a lot in the past and are still mistrusting of people in general, you may believe that nice is fake. Then, if someone is very nice to you, you'll assume they are fake or want something from you and poke and prod at this perfectly nice person who liked you until you were mean to them for no reason and pushed them away. When they've finally had enough, you'll be convinced that you were right to be skeptical because look, they up and disappeared *out of nowhere.*

Good judgment of character requires open observation. We all have biases, good and bad, but the more you can observe and allow information to come to you openly, the less you will try to flip to the last page of the story with each experience and slam the book shut on whether that's actually true or not. You never save time by rushing to judgment. If you believe a person is nice and innocent then nothing they do looks suspicious. If you believe a person is awful and untrustworthy then everything they do looks suspicious. Be very careful about assigning either of those judgments, because they are pretty certain once they're certain and don't leave much room for error once you start only seeing people as you believe they are.

4. Decisions – Decisions about your life are either going to be your responsibility or someone else's. Things don't just happen. Credit and blame go to the decisionmaker. From the most mundane to how you wear your hair and which shoes you should wear, to the most important like buying a house or taking a job across country, or should you marry this person, or have or not have children. All decisions have consequences. If you allow someone else to make your decisions, **you** will have to live with the consequences.

Even if they make a few good ones for you, that will only increase your confidence in *their* decision making skills, not yours, and because those results were so good you'll be more apt to ask them to make more and more decisions and become more and more a passenger of your own life. And if the decisions they make don't turn out, you'll be so angry and blame them for the consequences, not even acknowledging that you had a stake in the result and could have had a say in the decision.

We have to make decisions for our children when they are young because they are unable to make them for themselves. But once people are adults and know the relative rules of the game, it's better to encourage people to do what they think is right rather than tell them if they don't do what you think is right, they are wrong and an idiot. Even if sometimes they are wrong and an idiot. Some things, we learn by doing and only by doing. If you told someone exactly how to drive a car and they listened precisely to what you said, would they be a perfect driver their first time in the driver's seat? Of course not. They would have to take the wheel, learn to recognize the space around them, the sights, sounds, things they need to do or avoid, in order to become proficient. Of course, you may be terrified they'll have an accident, but if you encourage them and have confidence in them, you'll know that they'll get better over time and with practice and that fear will lessen in you. Learning means making mistakes. Making mistakes means learning. It's like a left and right foot taking steps. The only way to never make mistakes is to never learn, but if you do that, you never move forward on your own two feet.

Trusting Yourself in Bad Relationships

When it comes to a bad relationship with another person, you've got to trust yourself enough to know when you've only fallen in love with an image. You shouldn't wish that you hadn't seen, hadn't heard or overheard what shattered that image. Because that's like wishing for an illusion to continue instead of learning the truth and being able to decide what to do from there.

Integrity is usually thought of as affecting other people, but mostly it affects how you feel about yourself. If you are the only one who knows that your relationship that appears to be wonderful isn't true, then you will be separated from everyone else in your core group. You may even develop a subconscious incentive to try and fix that person so that no one will ever know you were in a bad relationship. Again, if you want to change something, you have to recognize it, and call it a bad thing. Otherwise, you're a willing imposter in the deceptive image. And when it finally ends, your friends will be so confused because you seemed so happy and they had no clue.

You may have heard of "imposter syndrome" where people who have good things happen to them don't feel they deserve it, but that's different. That has to do with self-worth and is about fear of actually loving yourself.

The duality of abusive partners can be like night and day. They may be charitable and seemingly selfless and kind to the outside world, but in the shadows, they are abusive people. How does that make sense? Their conscience weighs heavily on them so they try to polish and perfect the outer appearance instead of having the courage and honesty to look in the mirror and change. Maybe it hasn't even occurred to them that they should change. Their thoughts are so wrapped up in how to conceal and outrun the past and manipulate the future that they do not ever stop to even think about it. There's also a form of thought that if you've already done something awful you're already in trouble so you may as well keep on doing it until you're caught. That sounds ridiculous and it's so warped, but it's the way some people think. It's like they've given up on integrity entirely and have no sense that they have caused pain to others but they can prevent causing others pain in the future if they stop right this moment and come clean.

You know the expression "wolf in sheep's clothing?" It's a cliché for a reason. It can totally be that the monsters are people who appear meek and harmless or even Holy on the surface. That doesn't mean don't trust *anyone* who seems nice or is in a trusted position. It means don't rely on the fact that they have any certain job or title as if that would render it impossible for them to be any less than wonderful. Elaborate disguises are invested in and perfected by those who really want to hide the truth. You weren't stupid for falling for their disguise, and your friends and family weren't either. They invested in making it believable. If your friends don't initially believe you when it comes out, don't think they are against you. It is just hard to believe as it conflicts with everything they thought they knew and saw.

You have got to trust yourself and your own perceptions.

People who lie a lot don't at their core believe that they are good people, and they don't believe in trust as a positive and valuable quality of a relationship. Genuine trust just isn't in them so they don't see it anywhere in the world. They see trust from others towards them as a weakness to be exploited with the use of lies and fear. They believe you will only stick around if you need them and if you believe you have no other choices. So they exercise the abuse of your trust to create a need based loyalty and dependency so that they can try and get you to believe it's in your best interest to stay. They will even go so far as to tell you lies about what other people are saying about you so that you will believe you can't trust anyone except them. As if they are your only ally in the big, scary world.

Journaling can help you keep things straight and facts unchangeable. Your journal can be a critical resource if you're in a fragile state, feeling alone and enduring gaslighting at the hands of someone else. Examine your own motivations. Are you doing or not doing things because you actually want to, or because you are afraid of what would happen if you did or didn't? Gaslighting, if you don't know, is when someone deliberately manipulates, creates, and changes facts and says things with such certainty that you begin to question yourself. It is done to confuse and control. If you are ever in this type of relationship, seek support. Either from a trusted friend or professional support. It is so important to navigate your way out of it safely.

Calling it What it Is – No More Consolation Prizes.

You're only going to change in you what you call a bad thing. People don't do this often, though, and instead call themselves "too nice, too trusting, too loyal, too forgiving" and then think they should try to become *less of* those good things. Well nobody good wants to become less good. Those "too" phrases are consolation prizes – things you say to yourself to try to console yourself after you've been hurt. But if you do that, you're disempowering yourself and accepting that pattern which means it will happen again. And again. And again.

But what if instead of calling yourself, "too trusting," you called yourself, "too gullible?" That would identify a problem that you actually *want* to change. Something bad instead of something good. And what if instead of being mad at yourself for being "gullible," you took it one step further and realize that you are not really gullible, you just lack confidence in your own perception, intuition, and discernment? So the real issue is not "too" good of anything, but not confident enough in yourself.

That then clearly identifies what you need to change in yourself and that change will both break the old pattern and will make you a better person because you won't continue to enable people to play games with your mind or lie to or take advantage of you. You'll keep your power and control of your own mind.

Now, why don't you automatically trust your own intuition and discernment when something feels very off? Why do you try to talk yourself out of what you know inside to be true? It likely started and formed a long, long time ago. You were accidentally taught not to.

3 FORMATION OF TRUST: CHILDHOOD

When we are young, we trust fully. We even believe in the Easter Bunny or Tooth Fairy, just because we're told they exist. At some point, we find out about lies. At first, lying comes as a shock, but many come to accept it as a "normal" way of life. To trust, you have to have faith in the best in people. After your trust is broken many times, you may think that by not trusting, or by being skeptical, you'll not be fooled. But the true fool is the one who chooses to mistrust, as it never, ever, leads to happiness.

In childhood, the adults in your life are your pillars and role models. Literally, they are modeling the roles you learn that adults play in life. If they were not truthful, it really spins the way your perceptions form. Children assume adults know everything. Children trust so much and have so little worldly information that they believe in ridiculous things. They think adults know everything. For these reasons, if anything goes wrong in a child's world, they assume they themselves must be to blame.

With this in mind, think of the responsibility and burden a child feels when they are programmed with things like, "you make me so angry" and absorb it as if it were true. They become conditioned to believe that they, without intention, are the cause of other people's unhappiness.

The programming goes on to become your inner voice or conscience in adulthood, and to believe that if someone you care about is angry, it must be your fault and it is up to you to fix it. Change yourself until you no longer make them angry. Do more, ask for less. Ask for less. Ask for nothing. Smile and pretend everything is OK. Have no needs. Your survival depends on you not making them angry.

That is a direct action-consequence damaging dynamic but there is also a very common indirect action-consequence damaging dynamic that is done by adult parents who had only good intentions. The intentions are of protection and to shield their children from pain. The intentions are great, but the method is flawed.

Children are very perceptive, especially to their parents. Again, that skill is tied directly to survival. When a parent is upset, sad, or angry, the child will notice and inquire as to what is wrong. If the parent, with totally good intentions doesn't want to upset the child, the parent may say, "Nothing is wrong" and even fake a smile.

This is actually super damaging mentally to the child because the child now has a conflict of their perceptions versus their parent's stated reality.

This will cause them to doubt their own perceptions. Now, of course if you're upset that the mortgage is due and you're coming up short, you don't want to burden a child with things that are not their responsibility and are not in their control. But instead of denying anything is wrong, you can tell them that honestly you are dealing with some things that are your responsibility, not theirs. You can thank them for showing concern and even compliment them on their perception skills. This creates confidence in them, both in your word and in their own perception, and teaches them how to recognize truth versus fiction as well as a boundary definition that problems exist but they're not all theirs to fix. It also teaches them how to be honest and not lie about their problems or hide them in an attempt to shield someone else from pain. While still in childhood, that someone they learn to hide or not hide things from may be you. You're the last person they want to hurt. The honesty deepens trust and connection between you and them, and defines a loving relationship to them as one that has these qualities in it.

They will seek out similar dynamics in their adult life. Imagine the life altering repercussions of hearing, "This isn't your problem to solve" as a child. That defining statement that taught them their first major necessary boundary. It would tell them they can be caring and kind, but that doesn't mean extending into a guessing game of self-doubt and detective work trying to figure out and fix what is broken in someone else. By revealing that there is actually a problem, you're not exposing them to pain. You're teaching them that problems do exist, but that people get through them. You're not revealing yourself to be flawed and incapable, but rather to be human. You're teaching them it's OK to be that.

4 TRUST IN OTHER PEOPLE

If you believe in good versus evil as a rock solid either/or, then you are more likely to believe that you are good and people who seem similar to you are also good. Whether those similarities are your family, your church, your geographical area, your political party, your country, your sports team, your gender, or your race. This is also why it's difficult to manage when someone in one of these groups demonstrates that they are not that way. If you believe your identity is attached to that person or those people, there will be more of a tendency to hide or deny the awful truth if one emerges. Because in that black and white dichotomy, there are only two choices; and if they are part of the "evil," and you are attached to them, then you must be evil, too and you cannot accept that because you know it isn't true.

Also, if you believe in this dichotomy, you'll be more likely to toss people who look, act, or believe differently than you into the evil people pile.

Loads of problems here. Part of it is survival instinct, also known as tribalism. If we were all living in the wild, the loner would have a tougher time surviving. The strong group would be better able to survive and if one or some of the group members couldn't take care of themselves either temporarily or permanently, the other members of the group could ensure that they were receiving care and protection. The loner would either have to do everything for him or herself or die. So that's a pretty strong instinct. And the trouble with that is, it kicks in automatically whenever we feel threatened in some way. Fears, both real and imagined, can make people very mistrusting of anyone who doesn't fit within their tribe. Harmony cannot exist without trust. Unity amongst a population cannot exist without trust. This is why trust is critical for peace.

Trust in another person mean having confidence in their word. When you have trust, you have very little drama. You save a lot of time. You aren't questioned incessantly. You have peace within relationships. Trust is like air to a relationship. Without it, the relationship cannot survive. It must be valued and prioritized because with it, you have a mountain of confidence, but if it is broken, that mountain crumbles to dust.

When you learn something that was untrue from a year or even years ago in a relationship, it can send you into a tailspin because it revises your entire history of what you believed to be true and what was your reality. Many instances can be brought to mind as you re-evaluate and as your truth of reality recalibrates. Something important to note is that all that time, the entire time, the person who was deceiving you had a different truth that they hid from you. A whole other life story. If they were found out and did not come clean on their own accord, then their conscience never rose high enough to compel them to share the truth with you.

They are not the person you believed them to be.

The Law of Mirrors

In Happiness in Your Life: Book One – Karma, the Law of Mirrors was presented. It comes up in the topic of trust as well. You can only see what's in your mind. The motives you assign to actions are motives you assign in your mind. They may or may not be the actual motives of the other person. When you trust someone, you trust that their motives are good. When you don't trust them, even when it looks like they're doing something good, you'll likely question their motives.

One thing to really consider is your own mirror. If you are not really straightforward or honest about things you like or don't like, even if you're doing so in an attempt to be polite or not hurt someone's feelings, you're going to project that on other people. You won't take people at their word because people can't really take you at yours.

If you are straightforward and upfront, when questioned by someone on if you really mean what you are saying, you may get confused or even annoyed because you already answered honestly so what is the problem?

The problem is, they are not looking at you, but rather are looking at their own mirror. So to them, the truth is something in their own mind, and if it doesn't agree with what you've said, they will question it. Even if you again say the exact same thing, they may still hold on to the story that's in their own mind. This is why it's so crucial to use tact and kindness in honest conflicting or potentially disappointing opinions, but not make a practice of being deceitful even with good intentions. It affects not just that one instance, but if it becomes a habit, or was developed as a habit and continues, it affects all relationships negatively and prevents true connection because you're always questioning and inventing your own stories instead of being able to hear what other people are saying. "He says that, but I know he doesn't mean it." Or "You said that, but I could tell by the way you got quiet afterwards that you were really thinking this." Inventing stories is unnecessary and often faulty detective work and at the root of it is not trusting what another person says. Which, if they are actually a trustworthy person and are being honest with you, is confusing and hurtful and pushes them away. They will become frustrated that you don't seem to listen to them or believe what they say when they are telling the truth.

Trust Hierarchy

You will tend to trust certain people over others. For example in normal dynamics, you would trust your parents more than your acquaintances, and your spouse more than a stranger. In abnormal dynamics, you may trust people who you know less over people who you are committed to in life and see and speak with daily. This is usually when trust has already been irreparably broken but for some reason they still need to be a part of your life; for example a parent who has clearly demonstrated that they can't be trusted, but you want them to remain in your life.

This is also why in betrayal, which is deceit from those closest to you, you may be blind to things that appear obvious to others, or you may dismiss instances which would serve as proof positive to anyone else. Those closest to you who betray your trust may even use this hierarchy as leverage to be able to continue to abuse your trust and make you not believe someone not as close who is telling you the truth. Statements like, "You know me. That person is just jealous of what we have. Why would you believe them? They lie all the time, everyone knows that. I can't believe you're even asking me about this. I can't believe you even believed them for a second." They are trying to use guilt and turn it around on you in an attempt to shame you away from the lies they are attempting to hide.

This is also why you should not blame yourself if a giant, decades long deceitful betrayal is revealed. If you had no or only moderate trust for that person who was your spouse, you probably wouldn't have even been with them. The blame lies with the person who abused the trust given to them.

Misplaced Trust and Misplaced Mistrust

Trust is amazing, and is the basis of deep connection. But misplaced trust or misplaced mistrust can be very damaging. If you misplace trust, you basically write a ticket to being used, taken advantage of, and having your time wasted by someone who feels in control by being the only one who knows the actual truth. They build a wall around themselves with lies that create specific personas for all of the people in their lives. Whether they even know their true self is up for debate, because they spend all of their time focused outward, spinning plates to keep up all of the acts. Eventually, the webs of deceit unravel. Sometimes quickly, but sometimes not for years, decades even. Yes, you may have missed red flags or signs, but that doesn't mean you were stupid or did anything wrong. You trusted someone. That was an enormous gift to them which they did not value. In the future, to learn from this doesn't mean to close off and never trust anyone again. It means to trust people, but to trust yourself and your intuition as well.

Misplaced mistrust is similar, and often happens after you've been broken down by misplaced trust by someone else. If you haven't healed, forgiven, and released that awful experience, you may project it onto the next person or people who you attempt to be in any sort of relationship with. Because you were so hurt after being blindsided, you're now hyper aware of any hair out of place or anything that isn't exactly how it's supposed to look. Well, phones really do run out of battery and traffic really does happen. Not every action that's out of the ordinary or off plan means someone is a big liar just like the last one. If you are hyper-sensitive or not able to trust, it may be better to take any kind of relationship super slowly or focus on your own healing before attempting to get into one that has depth to it. You don't want to be someone who hurts and frustrates a good, trustworthy person because the wounds of a past relationship cut into the future. If you're unable to discern when it's not your intuition telling you something is wrong, but your fear of being hurt and deceived again causing you to become paranoid, it may be that you need to rebuild trust for yourself again first. It's not losing time to heal. And not being in another relationship quickly isn't your unfair punishment for what happened to you in the past. Once you've healed within yourself, you will be able to have a relationship better than what you may have ever experienced before. Even the person you choose will be different post-healing than one you would have chosen while you're still very raw and wounded.

Some people deliberately choose wounded people thinking they can be a hero and rescue and save them, but once the wounded person actually heals, they become disinterested because there's no hero job for them there anymore. When you enter a relationship from a whole and healed place inside, you will be attracted to a whole and healed person. That will be amazing. And we're not talking wait until you're 100 years old and have every sliver of pain resolved. That's not possible and you'd likely be the only one. There's a massive grey area between being not yourself but a broken paranoid version of yourself, and having healed to the point that you're not susceptible to becoming someone who you don't want to be as a partner. You're healed and whole enough when you don't feel you need someone to fix or complete you, or to make up for what another person did. When you can trust yourself, your own mind and discernment, and when you are seeking happiness and quality companionship in another person, not someone to rescue or be rescued by.

5 TRUST AND CONNECTION

Why should you trust someone you just met? Well, because they didn't give you any reason not to. They didn't do anything wrong. Everyone deserves a clean slate at the start. It's what you would want and deserve from another person, and it's what you should extend, too. Trust from the start is the only way to build a pure and deep connection over time. If a person then gives you reasons not to trust them, that will knock it down from 100%, but that's not something you can prevent by being closed off from the start.

When you meet a new person, whether it's a friend, at work, or a potential romance, it's your choice if you will be open with that person or closed.

If you are open, you begin from day one to learn about them and share about yourself. If you are closed, you withhold about yourself and apply judgment to what you see about them. We all start out being open with each other as children, often too open, over sharing or making honest observations that can sometimes offend. As we grow older, we experience pain as a result of being open and trusting people, and may close off to try to avoid that pain from happening again. Closing off doesn't prevent pain, it just prevents deep connection from occurring.

There are times in life where you are so wounded that you're not at the moment able to be open and trust, such as immediately or soon after an enormous betrayal. The wound is too large and has to heal before you'd be able to trust again, and to be yourself again. It seems tempting to shut off completely and vow to never trust again, but that's covering the wound with scar tissue instead of healing it. If that is the choice that's made, attempts at connection will be fraught with pain and regrets.

Instead of losing all trust in other people and in

yourself for being able to judge if a person is trustworthy or not, begin to develop trust in your own intuition, judgment, and most importantly, your own resilience. Some people practice for years at being skillful in deceiving others. No matter how many articles you read about how to spot signs of chronically deceptive people, a few are bound to deceive you, even if only for a little while.

Vulnerability

Vulnerability just means risk of being hurt. You cannot become completely immune to vulnerability, but you can reduce your vulnerability in a few ways.

Your best protections against vulnerability are;
1. to know, love, and value yourself,
2. to know what you want, expect, and deserve from any type of relationship,
3. to stay in the present moment with the person or in the situation,
4. to get to know them slowly and maintain your

life rather than 24/7 them on the brain—walk in, don't leap off a cliff,

5. to realize what is and is not your problem, job, or responsibility,

6. to know what is expected of you and to consciously agree to it or decide if it crosses boundaries, and

7. to fully accept that you cannot nor should not want to change a person or teach them as adults how to be better people.

Accept that they are exactly who they choose to be and respect their decision even if it means you're not going to be with them. Lying is about control and perceived safety by the one who is holding the strings, or the actual truth. Those who choose to do so as a daily method of life are attempting to be a puppet master, above and in control of the stories they create and those around them who they deceive into believing them. They think they are the master of the story, but really they are wasting everyone's time, including their own. If you, one character in their story, decides not to play along, they're not going to change the entire puppet show just to keep you around. It's best you make an exit and allow them to replace you with someone else.

Entering into a new relationship or job should be a case of "this looks great for both of us," not "oh help, everyone else in the world has let me down and you are the one who will rescue me." You want a peer, a mutually beneficial relationship, not a desperate vacuum chamber job of attempted rescuer which will only leave you more and more invested and depleted the longer you stick around. Some of these relationships can resemble parasites, with you, the host, thinking you're helping to bring another person up, meanwhile they are just going to take from you until there's nothing left to take and then move on to a new host. Sounds awful, and it is. You've got to value yourself and what you bring to a relationship and not allow yourself to be used. Reciprocation isn't selfish, it's normal. It's good. It's what a relationship should be. Each better off with the other than alone. Otherwise, why would good people ever want to get into relationships if all they were supposed to do was bring them down?

Connection is the most beautiful experience a person can have. Time is our most valuable commodity. We only have a certain amount of time here on Earth, and we never know just how much that will be. If we truly value our own time and the time of others, we can navigate away from situations that waste it and towards those deep, meaningful connections that make the most beautiful and worthwhile experiences in life come true.

Let's have a look at the Chart of Connection.

Chart of Connection – Doe Zantamata

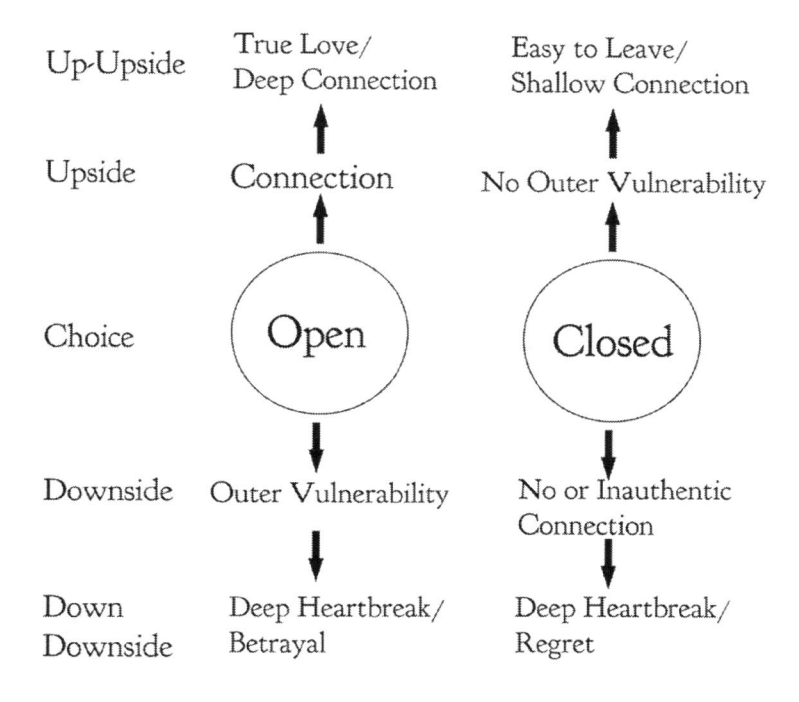

Up-Upside	True Love/ Deep Connection ↑	Easy to Leave/ Shallow Connection ↑
Upside	Connection ↑	No Outer Vulnerability ↑
Choice	(Open)	(Closed)
Downside	↓ Outer Vulnerability ↓	↓ No or Inauthentic Connection ↓
Down Downside	Deep Heartbreak/ Betrayal	Deep Heartbreak/ Regret

As you can see in the circles, your choice is to be open or closed. This isn't a one-time choice, but a choice that you engage in with that person or situation every moment that your lives are intertwined. There are upsides and downsides to everything in life, but as you can see, the downsides are really bad for choosing to be closed, and the upsides aren't all that great either. The top left quadrant is life's ideal – true love and deep connection - but you're only in control of your part; your choice to be open or closed. And again, the degree of the down downside of being open can be lessened or avoided by following those best protection practices against vulnerability outlined earlier.

To choose to be open means to choose to be free to enjoy life and experiences. To live in the moment and recognize that you don't have to have the entire road mapped out to be able to enjoy where you are. Each next moment is uncertain, and is an unguaranteed adventure. Things may change for the better or for the worse, but your awareness will allow you to adapt and either step in further or withdraw, depending on how things unfold.

Now, being too open too soon thinking that's a good thing is actually a big mistake and increases your vulnerability. If you are romantically interested in someone and after a few dates, you decide you want to be upfront and open about absolutely everything and tell them all about your deepest hurts and secrets, you may feel a weight off in that moment. But without knowing who they are, you may have just unlocked the door to your china shop for a bull to enter and destroy the place.

Honesty is a must, always, but full transparency is not for every person the wind blows your way. If you wouldn't give them a key to your house or your ATM card, don't tell them your secrets and deepest emotional pain.

A false belief is that if you share these deep things with someone, they will understand you better and know all you've been through and will treat you well and won't lie to you at all. But that isn't necessarily true.

A person is who they are. If they were going to lie to you and treat you badly, taking advantage of your pain, they're going to do that regardless of what you've told them, and you only made it a lot easier by exposing where your pain is. Doing so won't turn a jerk into a nice person. If you did open up fully too soon to the wrong person, you may feel a false sense of security from it, and be so shocked later and say, "how could this person do that to me **after I told them all that I have been through?!?"** Truth is, they were going to do it to you, or to anyone on their path. That's just what they do. By dropping your guard too soon, you threw away your protection. You don't go running around a bad neighborhood at 2 am with handfuls of $100 bills yelling "look at me! Someone stole from me before and it was awful!" and expect that because you announced you've been stolen from, that no one would dare do it to you again. If a person is going to lie, take advantage, or try to manipulate, they will try and do that. No matter what you do or don't tell them. If a person isn't going to lie, deceive, or try to manipulate you, they won't do it. Even if you don't spill all your secrets early on.

If you view uncertainty as a "fear" that you have and try and "overcome," you may lose or numb your ability to discern with your good judgment and intuition. If you instead see uncertainty as just *not yet knowing*, you won't give it that negative emotional charge. You'll be able to be open, aware, and optimistic, but with boundaries that are not based in fear. Boundaries will be the same as locking your front door. You don't lock it because you're scared of everyone. You lock it for protection and you choose who to unlock it for and allow in depending on if you want them to come in and trust them to be a good guest or not.

To choose to be closed basically means to live a shallow existence. It is easy to walk away from people and situations where you've never really invested yourself or connected, but that's really not a plus considering the point of life. It means you'll be forgettable, and you'll miss out on people who you could have shared some really beautiful moments with. The end result of a life of being closed is the ultimate down downside, regretting so many choices and opportunities for depth, but only realizing it at the end, when it's way too late.

This open or closed choice thing will be a brand, new concept for most people.

It's a pretty simple concept, but one that's going to take some time to put into practice in the real world. You do it all the time, daily in fact, when it comes to your daily goals. For example, if you want to go to the grocery store to get food, that is your goal for the **up-upside**. You get into your car, that is your **choice**. As soon as you step into your car and leave your driveway, you become **vulnerable** to the outer world because someone else could hit your car. That is a valid risk and is present every time you drive, but it's not the focus, nor should you try and feel great about it. It's just there. You deploy your **best protections** to reduce vulnerability, to lower the risk of accident. You follow the traffic laws yourself and stay aware of the other vehicles around you, even reacting and swerving out of the way if need be. You can never completely drop your vulnerability down to zero chance if you choose to get into your car. The only way you could have zero chance of car accident is to never set foot into a car again in your life. That would be choosing to be **closed**. But it would make life a lot more difficult if you never left your house just to try and avoid any type of accident out in the world.

People often talk about vulnerability or embracing vulnerability as if it's a good thing. Vulnerability is literally, just **the risk of danger of being wounded or killed**. You really don't want to numb the anxious feeling tied to being vulnerable and blast through it, because it could be your intuition trying to tell you that this experience is not right or good for you.

You also don't want to focus on the vulnerability aspect, because that act will *increase* the amount of anxiety you have about uncertainty in general.

For example, if you hear a knock at the door, you have the choice to **open** the door or leave it **closed**. Your only choice is to open the door or not. If you open it, on the other side may be your friend. Yay for opening the door, now you connect. Your choice was to be open, and the choice that was out of your control was his or her choice to be your friend. If instead you opened it and it was a robber, your choice to be open resulted in you becoming vulnerable to a robbery. The ways to reduce your vulnerability to a robbery would not be to embrace your vulnerability to a robbery, that doesn't even make sense. To reduce your vulnerability, you'd use your intuition, you'd peek through the peep hole, you'd ask "can I help you?" and "what would you like" **before choosing to open that door**.

Now another example, if you see a friend and you open your arms for a hug and walk towards them, you have **chosen to be open**. If they then also open their arms and you hug, you've **connected**. Technically, the moment you opened your arms, you became vulnerable or at risk for them to run up and punch you in the chest. The minute they opened their arms, they became vulnerable for you to run up to them and punch them in the chest. But neither of you had to embrace these vulnerabilities by saying "OK before I hug you I need to you embrace the fact that I could punch you in the chest here." Yes, it's *technically* a risk, but you don't have to embrace or acknowledge that risk before you connect with someone.

If every time you got into your friend's car, she said to you, "OK before you step in here, I need you to become crashable." Or if you got on a plane and the flight attendant said "Before you go to your seat, I need you to become crashable." Your first thought would be, "what on Earth is wrong with this plane??" For a plane or a car to crash, those are valid vulnerabilities, or risks. Cars much more than planes. But the risks aren't the reason you enter those situations. The goals are. To get to where you want to go.

Going further with that analogy, of course if you've just had a massive car accident, your fears of the vulnerability will likely be greater than they were before, but you don't then focus on those risks as you work through the trauma, you focus on getting back into the car and going places where you want to go.

Risk, or vulnerability, is present in life no matter what you do. Every time you eat, you become poisonable. When you are at your wedding day, the ceremony ends with "Congratulations, you are now married," ie, the goal. Not, "Congratulations, you are now divorceable." It is technically true that by eating you become poisonable, or by getting married you become divorceable, but you don't need to become OK with that fact every time you eat or spend a day being married.

Vulnerability is risk. That's all. It may or may not happen today or at some point in your life, but you don't need to try and feel honky dory about the possibility of being poisoned every time before you eat your sandwich, crashing every time you get in your car, or having your heart broken every time you choose to be open and connect with a person. You just live your life the best you can, experience it, and follow your best protections in all that you do.

The word "vulnerability" is used a lot in places it doesn't belong. Every time you see it, replace it with the words "risk of danger" and see if the sentence still makes sense. If it doesn't, that wasn't the right word to use.

And remember, taking time to heal after a deep betrayal isn't punishment. If you fell off a cliff, taking time to heal in hospital and physical therapy would not be punishment for falling off the cliff. Traumatizing relationships where trust has been demolished are akin to falling off an emotional cliff. You can't just magically heal the minute that relationship is over and leap right into another relationship because you deserve a great one. You do deserve a great one (if that's what you want), but healing takes effort and time.

You are only in control of your intentions and actions.

If someone seems to be consistently evasive when it comes to talking about their feelings or things that are important to them, it may not be that they don't trust "you," but that they just don't trust. It may be that they are not comfortable with anything deeper than shallow connections. This could be from being hurt in the past or just general fear. You can't make them open up, no matter how safe, kind, loving, or wonderful you are. It's a form of protection for them to stay closed. They don't know they're keeping the great out as well as the awful, but you trying to pry those doors open will only feel forced and violating and instead of opening them up, they may push you away entirely. Knowing what you want and what you are willing to give is one thing, being able to accept when someone you like does not want to reciprocate is another. There's no perfect day to determine this in the course of getting to know someone, but if you're feeling shut out after a few months or years have passed, you'll have your answer. You can't really regret what you didn't know as these things take time to unfold. Just make sure you're not hanging on to the hope of an investment paying off when you've never really had any indication that it was ever going to. You can't have a deep relationship with a shallow person. That's not an insult. Some people are perfectly fine and happy with shallow relationships for years, or even all of their lives. It feels safe to them. But if you want something deeper to feel fulfilled and connected, that isn't the place for you.

6 HOW TO BUILD AND MAINTAIN TRUST

From day one of a new connection, you are in the process of building trust. They may fully trust you with a clean slate as it should be, or they may have some residual trust issues that will prevent that. You may have the same. You can't really determine or control where a person is in their openness but you can control how you act and what you say.

Building and maintaining trust requires three things:

1. Honesty
2. Consistency
3. Clarity

1. *Honesty* is #1. If someone is repeatedly dishonest, you eventually won't trust a single thing they say. If you're honest in big things, little things, easy things, hard things, people will learn to value your word, even if it isn't always what they wanted to hear.

2. *Consistency* means that you *can* take someone at their word. Maybe not every single time, but most of the time. Inconsistency may not be a case of outright lying, but of indecision or being easily persuaded. This can look like the same thing as lying from the outside. It is very difficult to determine when you cannot trust someone like this, because when you speak with them, they seem so genuine in that moment. And they are. In *that* moment. But then they are just as genuine when someone else says something and they change to that opinion just as fast. "People pleasers" can often do this because they are fearful of disagreeing with anyone or any type of conflict. They will then inadvertently triangulate people and then

they will think they are the victim in the scenario they created because they were "just trying to make everyone happy."

Mistrust in someone's word is evident when you automatically don't really believe what they say. For example, if someone makes plans with you but repeatedly cancels last minute, with either valid reasons (especially if they are going through difficult times), or with not very valid, or no reasons at all. You'll eventually just not trust their word anymore and expect that they will cancel on you after it has happened so many times. What you do with that will be up to you. You can choose to not make plans with them temporarily if what they are going through is current but will pass. You may choose to be disappointed or angry every time and either tell them every time or hold it all in until you blow up at them for always wasting your time. You may take it personally and wonder why you're not important to them, when really, you may have made yourself the easiest to cancel on by seeming fine with it. You may decide to continue to make plans and have them be cancelled as no surprise and believe that this makes you a patient or understanding friend. You've got to do what feels right to you and what will resolve the problem for you instead of having it repeat. You can give them the benefit of the doubt and make them aware of it and then if they apologize, didn't realize they were doing this, and stop doing it, your trust will begin to rebuild. Outside of that, the solution will be something that is dependent on you, your decisions and your actions, not on trying to get them to change.

3. *Clarity* means without assumption. It also means without being silent when someone disagrees, which will look like agreement at the time if nothing to the contrary is stated. Then it will come out later that it was disagreement and the person will be very confused because why didn't you say something the first time it was brought up?

Lack of clarity means confusion and drama. We've all heard, "say what you mean, mean what you say." There's good reason behind that cliché! The opposite happens a lot!

You can't rush through building deep trust. It takes time to have different circumstances, situations, and experiences which will either build or break trust. You cannot see how someone will act or react until they are there in that moment. They may act or react the way you would have predicted, or entirely differently; worse or better. If it ends up being worse, you may wish you'd never experienced that because you're unable to like or trust them as much afterward, but truth is that's who they were before, you just couldn't see it until it was revealed with that circumstance. And if that type of circumstance is likely to repeat in the future, the way they reacted will likely repeat, too, unless they have undergone some deep reflection and have remorse about how it all went down. You've got to accept who and how someone is even if you wish that they were better and even if it would make things better for everyone. Even if you would have been there for them. Don't wish to unsee things, be glad you saw them when you did and not years and years of investment of your time and life later. If you've found out through circumstances that someone who you thought you were really close with was totally not there for you, trust has been broken. You can get mad at them, wish you could go back in time and somehow make them be there for you, regret being there for them when they were down because now you resent them for it, but all of that is non-acceptance of truth. You've got to be honest with yourself and put yourself in a better position to not have to rely on someone who has shown that they are unreliable to you.

Nobody likes rules, but here's 5 of them.

Five Unbreakable Rules for Unbreakable Trust:

1. *Honest doesn't mean fully transparent from the start.* If you've just met someone, you shouldn't feel as though you are being dishonest if you don't feel like opening up your life and tossing it all on the table. People shouldn't have to earn trust, but you should have some boundaries early on as the relationship unfolds. If a person asks a question that's too personal, you don't have to lie about it and then "come clean" later. You can assert a boundary that you think that's a bit too personal a question to ask someone they don't know. Remember, you wouldn't meet someone and hand them the keys to your car, house, and bank account PIN, so don't feel you need to hand them the key to all your secrets and to your heart on day one.

2. *Don't try to appear perfect.* If you don't know something, just say you don't know. If you made a mistake, say you made a mistake

and apologize. None of us know everything and we all make mistakes. What damages trust isn't the not knowing or the mistakes, it's how they are handled when they happen. If you try and pretend that you knew something or didn't make a mistake, you're attempting to fool someone. Whether they believe it or not doesn't matter, it's the fact that you will have just introduced deception into your relationship. Now if they don't believe it, their impression of you will change. They may or may not say anything in that moment. It is far more impressive to know someone who doesn't try to pretend to be perfect or deceive you than it is to know someone who does. Also, if you do the dance trying to pretend you didn't make a mistake when you did, then you also remove the opportunity to apologize. If you didn't do anything wrong, there isn't any reason to apologize, right? That also prevents a deeper connection and harms your integrity.

What's under this usually isn't an overt attempt

at deception. It's usually acting on fears and insecurities. Fear of looking stupid which is fear of not being good enough will make a person try to appear extra knowledgeable and perfect. Fear of being rejected means trying to become what you think they want. But acting on fears only brings them into reality. Then if someone does press you on something that was incorrect, you may feel disrespected or think that *they are trying* to prove you wrong or make you look stupid. But if you'd just said you'd made a mistake in the first place, that situation would never have come up. And if you are rejected, you may not even realize it wasn't because they didn't accept YOU, but that they didn't accept the bologna.

3. *Try to recognize when something similar isn't the same.* We've all been lied to and betrayed. We may be a little more touchy when a circumstance comes up that looks similar to one in the past with a different person. Of course you want to learn from your past pain and some things that look similar are

the same. But if you jump the gun and assign the guilty verdict too soon, it will put the other person into shock. If they are not guilty of the same thing, they will be hurt and will likely close off somewhat from you, or close off altogether. If they are guilty of the same thing, they may launch a manipulative defense and try to make you feel bad about over reacting which will stifle you in the moment but will make you question your own judgment later on down the road.

Observe and reflect, and try to stay unbiased but aware. Trust yourself, but also have compassion for those unhealed parts of you (we all have them) that may go into survival mode when there isn't actually an active threat. It's not easy. Especially if you're in the process of rebuilding your confidence and trust. But do your best. Have confidence in yourself and in your resilience and you won't be as scared to fall into a trap that you panic whenever a situation looks like it might be one.

4. *Be honest about the little things that don't seem to matter.* Sometimes people try to avoid conflict by telling little white lies to try and make themselves look better. Though they may seem little and insignificant, they can happen many times a day and turn into a really bad habit. They can also add up and erupt like a volcano later on when it's noticed that you "always" do them. If you're running 20 minutes late, don't say you're running 10 minutes late because it sounds better. If you don't really like something, say you don't really like it but say it in a kind way. If you're not really happy, communicate that instead of hiding it trying to please the other person. Assuming they don't want you to be happy and that they would rather you hide any disappointment or unhappiness doesn't say much about what you think of them. You may be accidentally setting them up to call them selfish later, but the truth is, they never knew because you didn't ever tell them. They took you at your word when you said you liked

something or were happy, many, many times. By not telling them, you're chipping away at the amount of trust they will be able to have for you when it finally comes out.

5. *Be Honest about the big things that do matter.* It's never a good time for bad news, but it's always the right time for the truth. The longer a lie is held, the more difficult it becomes to reveal the truth. If it's held a long time, two truths must be told; the original lie, and the reason it was held and covered so many times for so long. One becomes a thousand, and one is easier to forgive, and maintain trust, than many. Revealing is painful, but sooner is always easier, less painful, and better than later.

Jumping Off a Cliff Decisions

Well what an awful thing to call it, but that's the closest to what they are. *Jumping off a cliff decisions* regarding trust are seemingly small decisions that rapidly snowball into enormously tangled situations that can go on for years. With infidelity in marriages, the jumping off the cliff decision isn't the first time someone has physical contact with someone else. That is the inevitable result of a series of decisions that were not even attempting to maintain trust in the primary relationship. The casual flirting, the text messages, the smiles and glances, those all built and led up to the affair. Once those were set in place, the momentum had already begun.

Or in business, the jumping off the cliff decision is the decision to steal or cheat a little, even under the guise of "just this once," or "they have plenty of money, no one will notice," or, "I'll pay it back." Once that first deception has occurred, that weird repeat phenomenon happens; the one where people think, well, they're already in trouble anyway so they may as well keep going until they are caught. Their goals then don't become to have remorse or come clean, but to keep getting away with it.

Especially if they got away with something once or twice and it was very easy, they can tend to convince themselves that it's not bad and doesn't hurt anyone. Once they've convinced themselves of that, the gates are open until someone else catches on and closes them.

What to do?

Well, consider every decision that gives you pause. That pause and uneasy feeling is your intuition telling you not to jump off this cliff. "Would you like to go for a drink?" in and of itself can seem innocent enough, but if you have that uneasy feeling but go anyway and then lie about it to your partner later, that could very well be your cliff. Consider your integrity and if you'd do what you are doing in front of your partner. If not, then don't do it if you value the relationship. Even if it seems exciting and gives you a rush of dopamine. Do what you'd have done to you. Otherwise, someday it will come back to bite you.

As far as business, don't steal! Period! Stay honest and you won't hurt people. Stay honest and you'll never have to worry about a day that comes when you're found out. Stay honest even when it looks like crooks are getting away with way bigger things and it's easy and doesn't seem to matter. Stay honest and any success you have will be both rewarding and deserved.

7 ALL ABOUT LYING

Why Do People Lie?

People lie for basically only two reasons:

1. They do not believe the truth is good enough
2. For a short-term, self-centered, perceived gain

Alternative Ways of Lying

Someone can be lying but it may not be as easily recognizable if it's not a statement that is 100% directly untrue and opposite of fact.

Alternative forms of lying set up frustrating patterns for the liar which *they* will get mad about, without even realizing they are the ones who set them up.

1. **Playing Dumb** – Pretending not to know something is wrong. The recipient of the playing dumb lie will then explain right and wrong to the liar and will begin to assume the liar isn't very smart. The liar will become frustrated with the recipient and exclaim, "what do you think I'm stupid?" or that they are condescending, misogynistic, or emasculating if they attempt to explain other obvious things with good intention.

2. **Faking Memory Loss** – "Oh, was that today?" "I'm sorry, it slipped my mind." Yes, people really do forget things and no, not every time someone forgets something were they actually deliberately avoiding it knowing that they'd pretend to forget later on. But if they keep happening to forget dates, events, times with you and don't seem to forget much else or make any extra effort to remember things in the future, it could be that they're not forgetting at all. It's not your responsibility to chase after grown adults and remind them several times about things they could just as easily remind themselves via writing them down or setting up notifications on their phone or computer. Again, you've

got to watch your compassion here because if you are being manipulated but then think they actually are suffering from memory loss, you may overexert yourself trying to help them and later be told off for micromanaging or controlling them. Stay aware and objective and you'll be able to see things a lot more clearly.

Claiming to Fear the Truth

"The truth will set you free" but the truth always keeps you free.

When people who lie claim they fear telling the truth because they fear the consequences of it, that is also untrue. They may have residual phobias about parents who were very controlling and wanted them to think the way they thought and were punished when they didn't. But to recreate that dynamic in adult peer-to-peer relationships will only turn them into the frustrated and angry child again, alternating between being very agreeable and rebelling against their partner when their self-created resentment makes them exclaim that they've "had enough." This comes as a shock to the partner who was in the dark the whole time and thought they had good communication and got along well. They've been projected as the parent this whole time and are now being cast as the unwitting villain in this person's victim story.

Some people say they choose to hide things and be falsely agreeable to "keep the peace." But it's really creating future drama and avoiding healthy conflict resolution. People are different. We have conflicting desires, wants, and needs. We have different opinions. When we are close with another person as in a partnership, we communicate these things to each other and even in identical twins, there's no way they will ever match up 100%. So, there is the need for healthy conflict resolution. This involves how important the issue is to each person, if the two can find a mutually agreeable solution even if it's not what either one wanted in the beginning, and honest communication about what is or is not OK moving forward.

Unhealthy conflict resolution means avoiding it and being falsely agreeable or one person always making all the decisions in a controlling manner. The latter is what the falsely agreeable person thinks everyone is, whether they are in reality or not. Until they realize their role in the creation of this dynamic, they will just repeat the pattern with the same person or different people. There is no other option.

Another group of people who claim to fear telling the truth are people who actually fear the consequence of lies but still tell them anyway. The **truth** and the **truth revealed after a lie** are two entirely different things.

And yes, if a person comes clean about something there are going to be more questions. Like, "why did you feel the need to lie about that?" or "is there anything else?" This puts an uncomfortable consequence spotlight on the person who has come clean and they may mistakenly believe that this is what happens when the truth is told. No, that is what happens when lies are told.

The lie seemed to have afforded an escape from consequence at the moment it happened and the truth coming out seems to hold all the consequence at the moment it happens. The easiest way to avoid all of this nonsense is to just tell the truth from the beginning.

Forgiveness Versus Trust

Forgiveness is about the past and only the past. Forgiveness is letting go of resentment towards a person or event. But if you have forgiven someone, it doesn't mean that everything in the present is as it was before. If trust has been broken, that trust needs to be repaired. You're not an unforgiving person if you don't automatically trust someone after they've broken your trust. That's putting blame on the wrong person and them refusing to accept responsibility for their own choices.

An apology doesn't come with an eraser. Forgiveness doesn't mean memory loss. Once the house of trust is broken, it has to be rebuilt. Things aren't the way they were before, and they may not be for some time. If the person who wasn't truthful isn't willing to be patient and open to rebuild broken trust, then it may not be possible to rebuild.

This is particularly important when dealing with people who are addicted to drugs or alcohol. In these cases, it's better to say "people who" and the lying behavior rather than labeling them as liars. Lying is part of addiction. In physical withdrawal, it feels like life or death to not have drugs or alcohol and the person who is addicted would likely say or do anything in that moment to get the money, drugs, alcohol so that they no longer feel like they're going to die. It's not about lying for the sake of lying, but as part of the real problem, the addiction.

With your best efforts and patience, you may be able to help them some, but only they can fix themselves. If it's turning you into a nervous wreck then even though you'd love to help, you may have to set that ideal down and take care of yourself by creating some distance. It just may be that distance becomes the signal to them that they need to change if they want to keep a great person around.

Whether addiction is the cause, or pathological lying, physically/mentally/emotionally abusive, or cheating, all of these behaviors are often chronic rollercoasters in relationships. These behaviors are symptoms of deep pain. You can see a good person inside them in glimpses, and you so want to trust them and help them get through so you believe them again, and again, and again. Then when it comes out they've done it yet again, this is going to throw off your whole perception of and trust in yourself as a good decision maker. They LOOKED so remorseful! They had genuine emotion in their eyes and practically BEGGED for another chance! They PROMISED!

Now, if you think to what's common of all of those behaviors, it's not really truth versus lies, but control versus no control. They want to control the truth that they have (ie, the whole truth), and the truth they want you and others to see (ie, partial truths).

What you were actually seeing when you threatened to leave was not their genuine remorse, but their genuine fear of loss of control.

In that moment, they would say anything to prevent losing that control over you.

But then if you agree to stay, that moment passes.

The threat is gone.

Worse yet, after that moment passes, they will resent you for "making them" feel the fear of loss of control and for threatening their perceived stability. They may even become determined to get back at you for hurting them and for having power and control over them with "your threat" to leave.

You believe you are staying for them and to give them a chance, but they believe you are awful to them for threatening their security and *you* are trying to control *them* with your threats. If this is the case, you'll be able to recognize it. They will become paranoid and go on the offensive towards you, but believe they're acting defensively. They won't make any efforts to actually follow through with any of their revelation moment promises, and they will become annoyed and angry with you if you dare even ask them about those unfulfilled promises.

If a person believes they should not have to do anything differently or be more transparent until your trust is rebuilt, you'll be at a roadblock.

The ball is not in your court to accept the consequences of their actions.

If you try to pretend everything is fine and they refuse to do anything nor feel they need to, the pattern will repeat. If they pretend not to know what they did wrong or dismiss, diminish, or twist things to divert responsibility, the pattern will repeat. If they show no remorse or the deception went on for a long time until it was found out, the pattern will likely repeat. If they get mad at you and say, "Aren't you over that yet?" the pattern will repeat. If they throw guilt your way and say, "you're just like everyone else," "you said you'd accept me as I am," "I had no idea you were such an unforgiving person!" "I'm doing my best! (when they are not)" or "you promised you'd never leave," "you never loved me!" or other attempts at making you feel as though you have to prove something to them, the pattern will repeat.

You are not wrong for not trusting someone to be in your life after you've forgiven them if they show no sign of remorse or trying to make amends or accepting responsibility for doing so.

It takes patience, time, transparency, and honesty to rebuild trust after it has been broken.

If they're mad that their life has changed and they are expected to be more of those things then they are mad at their own consequences and should have made better choices so they wouldn't have to face them. All they had to do was be honest and decent and they wouldn't have broken your trust. Do not take blame for their actions.

"Sorry" isn't a magical get out of consequences word. Trust can be repaired and rebuilt, but a person has to commit to and want to do so. If they don't, it will likely be a deal breaker for any chance of a healthy relationship. Yes, it's too bad and if you were even willing to stick around while they rebuilt your trust for them, you already extended yourself more than you had to. If they don't even recognize that, then that is not in your control.

Conversely, rebuilding trust when it's been broken is not only dependent on the person who has broken it, or how many times they can prove they will be honest. It depends on the person who has had their trust broken. If you choose to try and trust again and if you are gradually able to, the relationship may be worth another try. If you are not able to trust again at all and would be in a constant panicked or anxious emotional state, the relationship has no hope of survival and should be ended. It's not your fault if that's your choice. You didn't break the trust and the relationship. You just decided that once broken, you don't believe it can be put back together. That is your option and a valid one if it is what you truly believe.

Interpretation and Perception – Liar Immunity

The worst thing about lies is that they cause a person to doubt if they should trust so much. But the problem isn't too much trust, it's too many lies. Recognize when you can't trust a certain person anymore but don't let that spill over to all people. You'll never find true connection at arm's length, but if you put up a wall of mistrust, that's the closest anyone can ever get.

If you're *not* a person who lies all the time but *are* tired of being duped by people who do, you don't want to trash the amazing quality of trust and turn into an expert detective and interrogator. You do want to develop your **Liar Immunity**.

What you need to do to develop this skillset is of course a learning process like most everything else. It involves changing some methods and habits you have that you have, up until now, thought were good qualities.

There are 10 Ways to Develop Your Liar Immunity and Resilience

1. Give the benefit of the doubt, not the benefit of no doubt.

Giving the benefit of the doubt is a good quality. But overdoing giving the benefit of the doubt means to turn a blind eye to reality and that will always come back to bite you. Being positive does not mean only seeing the good (especially if you have to make it up). If someone is acting odd, or is late, or doesn't call or text back, just ask why. Don't create a positive *benefit of the doubt story* for them to simply agree with. If you have already created a story, it doesn't take any lying skill to just agree. You're making it much too easy for them.

For example,
Reality: Spouse is out cheating and comes home late.
You: Oh, did you get stuck in traffic?
Spouse: Yes.
You: I tried to call you, was the reception bad?
Spouse: Yes.

Later…

You: Oh my, they were SUCH a GOOD LIAR! I didn't have a clue!

No they weren't. All they had to do was agree with the stories and excuses you provided them with. **You were actually the good liar!** But now it's coming as a shock to find out they are not who they never were.

How do you go about it instead?

Ask!

And if they have a simple answer, super!

Example:

You: Why were you late? I tried to call you, but your phone went straight to voicemail.

If they immediately leap into, "what are you accusing me of?!?!" well that's a sign of someone trying to scare you off from the truth. Don't fall for that. What they want in that moment is for you to feel bad, to apologize to them for "accusing them," and for you to back off.

Instead, you can calmly say, "I'm not accusing you of anything. I asked a simple question." and wait for their reply.

If they can't answer a simple question and go on about how they feel interrogated or their ex didn't trust them and questioned everything they did (a distraction tactic to try and make you want to be better than the ex), just stay aware and objective. If you can't ask a simple question without being railroaded, this may not be the place for you. Would you act that way if you were late or if your phone died and they couldn't reach you? Reverse the roles in your mind to see things more objectively. Doing this can make things become very crystal clear when something is way off.
Simple questions have simple answers.

If someone says one thing then says or does another or the opposite, there may very well be a logical reason. If you ask and one is provided, it's probably true. But you have to ask. No speculating with friends or creating a drama story in your mind.

Just ask.

If you do ask and their response is either angry that you're accusing them of something, or massively evasive/subject changing, or over explanation with loads of unimportant details, you have reason to be suspicious.

It could very well be that they use lying as a mechanism to build an image that they wish others to see. If you question them, you are in effect chipping away at that image, that armor, and the very act of asking a simple question will be perceived as an attack on them. They want you to see what they show you, not the truth.

It is hard sometimes, especially if your trust is already in recovery, to discern if you are actually being paranoid and reading into things versus when you're dealing with actual lies. But the answer isn't to shy away from saying anything altogether. Communication is a part of healthy connection and trust. If you can't communicate, then both trust and the relationship will eventually go down the toilet.

Without communication, the most you have to go by

are actions and assumptions. If it's important to you, make an extra effort to talk to the person or people directly. Then use your intuition and logic to make sense of the whole thing. You can't make a whole decision on partial information.

2. Believe that the truth will always find you

Start to believe that the truth will always come and find you. Really believe this. Say it as an affirmation first thing in the morning and last thing before you go to bed. Rewire your brain to have confidence in this as a fact. It's not magic, you'll just become open to seeing it wherever it is. You'll also be more perceptive to signs you may have otherwise missed entirely. They will sometimes seem like totally random series of events that lead the truth to you and it will look like magic, but really it's just the way things work and most people are unaware of it, so they never see it until they look in hindsight after finding things out in other ways.

Plus, liars let their guard down when they don't think anyone is watching them. If you are just relaxed and open, their most idiotic lies will fall into your lap and you'll be able to see them so clearly without ever once having to play detective.

First bliss comes naturally. Second bliss is a choice. It's the choice to trust, to love, to put yourself out there, knowing full well that you can get hurt. But you won't be able to live, love, and experience all the joys of life if you don't put yourself back out there again. It takes courage – a lot of courage – but it's worth it. Have faith in yourself.

3. Receive the Truth When it Comes to You

When the truth does show itself to you, don't deny or dismiss it because you really like who the person appeared to be. Know when something is gold versus gold plated, and when the veneer is lovely but the wood underneath is rotten. If you try to pretend or excuse away things, you will be very frustrated with yourself later on when you look back at the red flags you ignored.

The longer you're in something, the more invested you become. The more invested you become, the more difficult it is to leave because you don't want to feel like you've lost your investment.

People also deny what they see and know because they believe that being duped or fooled by someone makes them stupid or gullible. Rather than face self and outer humiliation or judgment for being stupid or gullible, they become another actor in the con's theater. To the con, they may try to change ("help") him or her, or they may just avoid any confrontation at all and pretend not to know.

Denial isn't *being positive*.

Denial can go on for years or even decades and the damage keeps getting more and more difficult to sweep under the rug. It doesn't fix itself. It often becomes worse and worse over time as the deceptive person realizes they don't face any consequences. They become bored with their current level of deception and increase it for more excitement, or more of a challenge to see what they can get away with. They view it as a form of power, like a puppet master, holding all the strings.

Not seeing things is one thing, but not wanting to see things and trying to pretend they are different than they are is lying to yourself. If there's no problem, there's no problem that can be fixed, and what is broken remains broken until it gets to the point when it's absolutely undeniable. At that point, it may be too late for salvage, let alone repair. Don't wish you still didn't know so you could remain in ignorant bliss.

Be grateful to have learned the truth and use your courage to address it.

4. Realize that Scolding and Catching People in Lies Does Nothing to Stop the Lying

Remember, people lie for only one of two reasons (because they don't believe the truth is good enough or for a short term, self-centered, perceived gain). Neither of those reasons is cured by catching someone in a lie. In fact, it can do the opposite. If they are lying because their intent is to manipulate or try and look better and feel smarter than you by outwitting you and fooling you, then you catching them in a lie makes them feel stupid. Worse than that, they were lying in an attempt to control the narrative. Now that they've been found out, they feel a panic as they've lost control. This is also why pathological liars absolutely freak out when they find out when someone has been lying to them.

You'd think knowing how it feels to be lied to would make them stop, but that's assuming empathy. They see it as a competition and if they've been lied to, they lose. If you don't believe their lies, they lose. They do not want to lose. The last thing they're going to do is realize there's no point to lying.

They will see it as a challenge to fool you and prove that they are smarter than you. It's warped logic, and definitely not what you'd be looking for in a partner. It's a belief that you are against them and they have to be in control of what you believe is true to keep you around and keep them feeling like they're holding the reins.

5. Practice Acceptance

Acceptance doesn't mean accepting lies and sticking around in the same capacity. That's willful denial. Acceptance means accepting that this is what they feel they need to do to survive in this world and that you cannot change that. You can only continue to be subject to it, or distance yourself enough that you're not. If you'd like to believe that they're just fearful of the truth not being good enough and maybe as they know you they will be comfortable being truthful with you, then set a number of lies you will tolerate. 1 more? 10? 25? You set the number and then put it out of your mind. Make that your personal boundary. If they cross the threshold that you set, leave. That boundary has to be firm otherwise it becomes a slide into an abyss of deception. The more "chances" you give them, the less your word means when you say you're going to leave, and the less they will actually respect you because they know they can just plead and cry for a minute and make some promises and you'll stick around. "I didn't mean to hurt you" only works with accidents. Lies are not accidents. Eventually, they'll even stop apologizing at all and turn it on you because they'll tire of getting in trouble and will become frustrated that they can't fool you. They'll say you're nitpicking, or that they do a lot of good things, or everybody lies about "that," and you're overreacting, or a whole slew of other things that are a stark difference from the first few times. You are neither their parent, nor their counselor but that will be the dynamic that is created. It's supposed to be peer to peer, equals. It's not that hard to just tell the truth, really. Don't you deserve someone who respects you and values your trust enough to be honest with you?

6. Always be Direct and Straightforward

First, remember, there is a difference between honesty and transparency. The closer a relationship is to you, the more your and their words and actions will determine your decisions and things that affect your life and vice versa. The closer a relationship is to you, the more transparent it needs to be. The further or more distant a relationship is to you, the less transparent it needs to be while still remaining honest. A nosy neighbor shouldn't hear about complaints your spouse has about you at all, let alone before you do. If and when it eventually gets back to you, you will feel humiliated and your trust for your spouse will be damaged. Plus, the neighbor can't do anything about it anyway.

If it is important enough to bring into words, those words should be directed to the party involved for resolution. By bringing them to someone else; the neighbor, a friend or relative, only one side of the story is being presented for judgment which will probably be agreement because of how it's presented. That will then increase the divide between the two parties that it actually involves, and fuel unnecessary drama and pain by including someone else. And if it is resolved between you and your spouse, you'll still harbor resentment to the third party and the third party will harbor judgment towards you.

Always assume that people cannot understand your perspective and feelings unless you've explained them to them. What is so clear from where you stand may be completely invisible from a different perspective. If you do explain and they still don't get it or just don't care, then it doesn't mean you've wasted your time. It just means that you now know for sure that if you value being understood or considered, this won't be a person who can do those things very well if even at all.

7. Trust Your Intuition

Don't make up excuses or reasons for why your intuition is giving you a signal that things are wrong. Evaluate the feeling. Meditate on it. Maybe it is just your own past pain from being lied to coming back to haunt you in a moment of doubt. Maybe there's not enough information to make any solid decisions just yet, but don't ignore it or try to dismiss it. If things don't feel fine or if a person's words don't match their actions, trust yourself to know the truth. Sometimes it can be difficult to determine if it's your fears from past pain or actually your intuition telling you to close off or be skeptical. Intuition feels more like a repulsion or uneasiness, whereas fear feels more excited and nervous. But moving forward full steam ahead while in great fear is not a good energy to bring to decisions, either. Those decisions will tend to be more irrational and snap decisions.

Taking some time to address your fears and determine for yourself if they are rational or irrational based on present day circumstances can alleviate some of the fear so that you can see more clearly and with less bias. It still takes some courage to trust yourself and your intuition to remain open in the presence of fear. A little to moderate fear popping up is normal. Fear exists naturally when it comes to deeper relationships because you realize at some point that you're walking on a wire with no net beneath you. If the person on the other end decides to snip the wire, you're going to fall and it's going to hurt. That is exactly why placing your full trust in another person is such a gift.

8. Observe

Does this person lie to other people all day long? Do they say, "it makes things easier" or "it looks better?" When faced with semi-awkward situations, do they face them truthfully or try to think up schemes and say things like, "I'll just say that.." and make up stories as excuses which they know for a fact are not true? Or justifying lying as if it's as logical as breathing. For example, if you ask someone why they just lied to someone else, and they dismiss it with something like, "Oh, well I just said that to avoid an argument." Or, "I just said that to get them off my back," or "Well YOU KNOW I don't mean that." You've probably heard that people who gossip to you also gossip about you and that goes for lying, too.

They may tell you that you are their confidant or the only person they can be honest with, but without a doubt, if they're lying as a means of living to everyone, they are lying to you, too. "But how could he or she lie TO ME?" Habitual liars lie. That's how they operate, and they don't know how to function without it. They see it as a means of control and power in their lives and as an armor of protection.

You cannot change that. Lying about things that are so small or insignificant is a really bad sign. It shows that this person incorporates lying into their daily routine and they feel power in creating realities that they want other people to believe. They are the only ones who know the truth. While they think it gives them power, it actually only isolates them into a world of one. Worse than that, knowing that people believe they are a better person than they know they really are isn't a fun world to live in at all. There's a lot of self-created pressure to keep up the act. Remember that actions speak louder than words, and the old story that ends, "who you gonna believe, me or your lyin' eyes?"

9. Take Things Slow in New Romances

When dopamine is kicking in the excitement of a new relationship with someone you like a lot, it's easy to get swept up and dive headfirst into the deep end. But doing so may have you diving headfirst into painful rocks that you couldn't have seen from the shore. Wade in, maintain your life and friendships, and allow yourself time to get to know someone. Everyone can be dazzlingly charming for a few weeks or even a few months. True colors come out a little after around a month and more after around three months. It's not possible to maintain a flawless act for longer than that. If indeed it was an act, you won't be stuck or confused as to what happened or did you do something wrong when the person changes dramatically into someone you haven't seen before and really don't like. People who put on acts invest a lot of energy into them and begin to resent you, the audience, for "making them" perform. You didn't ask them to nor were you even aware that's what was going on, but to them it's still your fault. Signs of this can be subtle, like they'll suddenly not like things you like that they already said they did a few weeks before, maybe even enthusiastically claiming to LOVE those things, "too."

10. In New Romances, Ask an Important Question

Ask them why their past relationships ended. Not in great detail, but just to see the answer. If they claim all their exes were the devil incarnate and they were the faultless victim, that is a giant red flag. Likely, you will be the next devil, even if they claim you're the first, best person they ever met. The pedestal may feel flattering for a moment, but if their story is that they are the only good one and their chosen partners are the bad one, you've got to be the bad one. It's the role they've assigned to partners. It means they haven't accepted responsibility for or grown through their relationships and that you will be the next devil created by their own projection no matter how kind or nice you are. If you're unaware of this, it can be a steep fall from the pedestal and one that hurts. You may be sucked in and tempted to try and climb back up on the pedestal but by doing so, you'll only lose yourself on the way.

8 BREAKING TRUST WITH GOOD INTENTIONS

Not every instance of breaking trust has bad intentions. Not every lie is recognized as being a lie.

Fears can play into the poor methods chosen;

1. low self-worth and fear of not being good enough to be liked,

2. fear of rejection, or them liking you less,

3. fear of hurting someone's feelings,

4. fear of disappointing someone,

5. trying to avoid conflict.

But as long as these methods are being viewed as good things, they will continue. And as long as they continue, the pattern of pain will repeat.

Right when you first meet someone who you like, you may be so caught up in being happy and liking them that when they ask you about things that you can do together, you're not honest with them about what you don't really like or don't have any interest in. Not because you were deliberately lying, but because you were happy and happiness is such a great feeling and you didn't want to risk disappointing them by disagreeing with them. Having a lot in common is highly valued between two people when they first meet as a form of connection. But if they truly are a good person who is interested in you, spending time with you, and doing things you both enjoy, they are asking you these questions to determine your future plans together. The last thing they want is to be told *yes* when it's actually *no*. That defeats the purpose of asking the questions at all.

And what it means for you is that somehow you have tied your dishonesty to their happiness and you only say what you really mean or how you really feel when you are fed up or angry. If you've set things up this way, you will eventually feel like you're not being considered when they believe they've been choosing things you both like this whole time because that's what you told them. And if you then justify not being honest by saying you didn't want to hurt their feelings by saying you didn't like something they liked…well you'll probably actually hurt their feelings by not being honest with them.

People can like different things and have different opinions. Different doesn't have to mean "wrong." What they or you like that the other doesn't like is just a difference in opinion. Everyone has different tastes and shouldn't ever feel bad if those tastes are not the same. You may think yourself to be an honest person, but if you're doing this – even with good intentions – that is dishonest, and you are eroding their trust for your word.

The trust that is then broken has more consequences. If you get fed up and tell them you're sick of only doing what they want and then are reminded you said that's what you wanted, too…you may not be able to see that this is your creation. And then in the future if they're gun shy from being blown up at, they may ask you if you'd like to do something or go somewhere and if you say "yes," they may ask you if you're sure or if you're just saying that. If you still haven't realized your role in the creation, you may see this as a separate issue and get mad at them for questioning or doubting you when you've already said yes.

By being honest, you will cease to set people up to be the bad one later on down the road after you've created a backlog of all the things you've done for them to "try and make them happy."

Being dishonest with people hurts their feelings. Being dishonest with people doesn't make them happy.

An honest frown is worth more than a million

phony smiles. Pretending to be happy in an attempt to not disappoint others will only leave everyone unhappy in the end. Expressing feelings honestly is the only way to resolve differences and create truly happy surroundings.

How do you change the habit?

Learn to be able to say things other than yes when you don't mean yes. It may feel awkward or uncomfortable as all those fears swirl in the back of your mind, but you will get better at it over time and with practice.

Instead of a false yes, you can say:

1. No

2. I've never tried that, but I'd like to since you like it

3. I'm not sure

4. I'm not really interested, but can we think of something else that we both like?

Having things in common is a valued form of connection, but even more than that is having honesty. Honesty, whether in agreement or disagreement, is an amazing connection and has so much more value than pretending to be in agreement.

You have to learn each other before you can know each other. In order to learn each other, you have to be honest from the start about who you are. We are also the most attentive at the very beginning, so not being truthful at this time can come back later on and damage the very first few stones in the foundation of your relationship.

Also, to know someone wants to try something new *because* you like it so much is of a much greater value than just pretending to like it, too. If they like it, too, it's a matter of chance. If they choose to do something different or step outside their normal world, they are choosing to grow with you. Isn't much more rewarding to choose to openly do this with each other than to hide things and pretend while developing resentment inside?

If you do this, you're far from the only one. In fact, many, many people do and think they are being polite and nice or easygoing by doing it and were taught that as little children and praised for doing it. It's a thing that needs to stop. You can be polite and nice and honest and easygoing and voice your disagreement all at the same time. And you have to if you want to foster and nurture true connections and be considered within them.

Accidental Breaking of Trust via Mountain Creation

Do you know that expression, "don't make mountains out of molehills?" Meaning don't make a big deal out of little things? Well a lot of people think they are doing that, but really they are building mountains from molehills. Don't make a big deal out of little things, but do make a little deal out of little things.

What am I talking about? OK, so let's go back to

that friend who regularly cancels plans with you at the last minute. You say, "It's OK," or "No problem," but really it wasn't totally OK and it was a little problem. Now maybe they give you a valid reason so you do understand but are still a little disappointed. It's good to express that. Recognize and acknowledge a molehill. Otherwise, you've created the foundation for a mountain and encouraged more to come. Now, if they had an emergency and they hardly ever cancel, of course don't toss guilt on them when you really actually do understand and it really is no problem. But other than that, what happens then is if they cancel again, or again and again because you've established yourself as the "no problem, it's OK" person, then all those molehills will build and build and they will have no idea. So then you may wonder why they don't value your time or prioritize your plans because they just cancel willy nilly after awhile and so you one day get fed up, maybe after years, and you tell them you need to talk. You present your case, with examples and theories and possible explanations and they don't respond well. At all.

Well they've just been blindsided! They really believed you when you said, "It's OK," and "it's no problem" and now all of a sudden they are on the jerk end of a story, woven over time without any indication that it was being formed.

So while you thought you were being nice and understanding, you were actually creating a storyline in which you will become the victim and they will become the bad guy. When this all finally comes out, they are recalibrating history and their trust for you in that moment will be broken. They will know they can't trust that when you say something is OK that it is actually OK. They may then question *you* further if you do say something is OK and really mean it, with, "are you sure? I mean are you really, really sure?" And if you're unaware of what you've created, you'll then get annoyed with them for questioning you and not taking you at your word because you believe you are an honest person.

The easiest time to be honest is in the beginning. None of that tension or resentment or anxiety will build around the topic. You can just ask, make someone aware, express how you actually feel. And maybe they won't receive that well and tell you that you are nitpicking and they are so much more easygoing. OK but they are not the one being cancelled on…so if they do react poorly then you can know that they are aware and choose not to change anything. That's an entirely different situation where you will likely then choose not to maintain your role in the dynamic because you know it's going to lead to disappointment.

Similar to this is trying to avoid conflict by withholding your true opinion, whether it be on politics, about an individual, idea, or circumstance. A lot of people fear conflict because it's been so associated with fighting. They think it's a good thing to avoid conflict. But, conflict just means disagreement. Unless you and another person are identical, you're going to have disagreements and conflicting opinions. The closer you are, the more they will arise. So if you don't learn how to resolve conflict in a healthy way, the longer you know each other, the greater the chance of division over time.

Consider conflict as an opportunity.

If you're only seeing your side, you're missing half the story. If you believe yourself to be good and truthful, then an opposite view instantly becomes bad and a lie. Compassion means understanding there is another point of view. Empathy means trying to see that point of view. Compassion and empathy dissolve anger through understanding. If people with two opposing ideas actively seek to understand each other, finding truth and resolve is not only possible, it's probable.

In this way, conflict can become an opportunity for personal growth as well as a deepening of connection and trust with another person. If you trust each other during conflict, you know that each is attempting to understand and resolve, rather than trying to be right and make the other wrong. Instead of arguing from opposing sides, you grow on the same side, together. If you avoid conflict and just agree, you'll be increasing the divide without the other person even knowing, and missing opportunity after opportunity to connect on deeper and deeper levels.

You are only in control of your intentions and actions. If the other person —whether a stranger or a close relationship – is only interested in winning and making you wrong and them right, or if they also wish to resolve with you is up to them. Unity is a much better way to build a healthy relationship, but you can't decide for them if that's what they want to do or not. You can only become aware of their intentions if you've tried to resolve and have been met with frustration when they still attempt to be right and "win" against you. If half a couple is a loser, the couple cannot win.

Friends Who Ghost

If a friend stops speaking with you because they made awful assumptions or believed gossip about you without even asking you "your side," then you didn't really lose a friend. You only lost a person who didn't trust or believe in you...and that's not really a loss at all.

It hurts because it feels unfair, and you would not have treated them the same way. But if that's the choice they've made, you can really only accept it and let them go. Even if you end up tracking them down and talking to them and convince them of the real truth in this instance, the breaking of trust will not have changed. Their decision was to not be open with you but go with their poor judgment instead. That will continue to hurt you in every future similar circumstance if their judgment remains cloudy even though the one instance was semi-cleared up.

9 TRUST IN THE WORLD, UNIVERSAL LAWS, AND GOD.

Trust in the World

If you believe that you are at a disadvantage or that everyone is out for themselves, you're going to believe that to get ahead in the world, you'll need to take from someone else, find a gimmick, trick people, figure out or learn a "trick" to beat the system.

You will see yourself as against the world and the world against you. One will lose and the other will win. And the only way to win is if someone else loses. Compromise means losing half the time. So many get rich quick schemes prey on these beliefs, but they are all false because they attempt an outside-in methodology which just doesn't work. Yes, you may fool some people or even a lot of people for a time, maybe even a long time. From a street corner hustler to a 40 year Ponzi scheme, it's all against you.

With this belief system, there is no room for growth, learning, and harmony. A better belief system to live with yourself and in this world is one were compromise means finding a solution where everyone wins, is heard, and is treated fairly. It's one where winning means unity among the couple or the group, with everyone feeling of value. It means believing there is good in you and in this world that hasn't been unveiled yet, but with time, honesty, compassion, and consideration, more and more beautiful treasures from the deep will make their way to the surface.

This is not a belief system for everyone. Not everyone has the strength to be that open, trusting, and positive. To those who are of the first set of beliefs, this will sound like idealist hippie nonsense.

Their concept of people and reality are so low that anything remotely good is regarded as riding on unicorns. You may be "gullible" to them for believing in good, but they're also gullible, but for believing in bad instead.

Everyone is gullible, or leans toward, or is vulnerable to what they already sort of believe. This is called "confirmation bias" and means basically that if your beliefs are a bucket, you tend to toss new information into that bucket and discard what doesn't fit or look the same. When presented with new information that is in line with what we already believe – good or bad – it is more readily and easily accepted because it already has a degree of certainty or trust. That then reinforces the belief even more. That's why people become more rigid in their beliefs as they get older. There's a lot more proof in their buckets.

When presented with something that goes against our beliefs – again, good or bad – about ourselves, other people, or the world, it is more highly questioned or outright denied and rejected more easily than it is accepted or even considered. This is called "cognitive dissonance." Fancy words that mean, "this doesn't agree with what I already think."

People tend to feel security in certainty and feel insecurity in uncertainty. Fear of the unknown or that things will become worse than they currently are if change is allowed to occur. But change occurs every moment of every day and much of it is not in an individual's control. From what happens on the news, to the weather. But rather than fear change, we need to learn how to adapt. Adaptation is a true survival skill.

It is good to observe and to learn, not just modify or accept or reject every bit of information or experience that comes your way. Keep an open and curious mind. Question your own beliefs, not to cast doubt or get confused, but to develop depth and confidence in your own judgment and discernment. Keep or develop the skill of evaluation and you will continue to learn throughout life.

Trust in God

Trust in God, or Allah, or a Higher Power, or The Universe, or any bigger picture. I'll use "Higher Power." Please translate it to the one you believe in every time you see Higher Power.

Disappointments and Rejection

When you trust in a Higher Power and do your best, you'll perceive disappointments and rejection differently. You'll know that "this isn't your door." Now, that's not to mean give up on anything that requires work or effort, but not to be so rigid in the way the path needs to unfold. It could be that your intention and what you are seeking seems like it would be found in that circumstance or person, but later you'll find out why it never would have been. For example, if you want to be successful and you apply for and interview for a job with a really great company but then they don't choose you, it may be that they are going to restructure or even close down soon in the future and getting that job wouldn't have turned out well for you in the long run. And of course in the moment of let-down, it will be natural to feel disappointed. But let those disappointments be replaced by your knowing, your trust that what's yours can never pass you by.

Now that said, what if EVERY good thing seems to not be your door? Well, it could be that you're missing one crucial part that doesn't have anything to do with trust but with self-worth. If you believe in good things, good people, good opportunities, but deep down you either don't believe that they can happen to you or that you deserve them, you may be subconsciously choosing ones that will end in disappointment to make those beliefs come true.

If you look back on things, circumstances, or relationships that you really felt so great about but then they dissolved or disappeared right before your eyes, what drew you into them? Did you feel worthy of them? Or did you really *want* them but not actually feel *worthy* of receiving them?

Energy sometimes speaks louder than words. If your energy in the face of connection was suddenly self-sabotaged by self-doubt, disbelief, or unworthiness, that energy will be palpable to everyone you are about to connect with. The employer, the potential partner, or even the friend. They may not be consciously aware of what has changed, just that they don't have the good feeling they did before. All of a sudden the spark disappeared or this just isn't working out.

In order to trust your Higher Power to bring you the good things you deserve, **you've got to believe you deserve the good things**. Otherwise, you may as well trust your Higher Power to bring you the disappointments and rejection no matter how good you are or how hard you try.

Think of how you received the last few good things you received. Whether it was a gift, a compliment, a promotion, or a lucky break. Did you receive them openly and with gratitude? Or were you hesitant, skeptical, or outright reject them? Did they seem "too good to be true?" Really evaluate your own past actions and then think of how you'd expect a good person you know to respond if given the same good things. Think of how you'd expect a good, deserving person to respond if you were to give them the last few things you were offered. This is hard. It's hard to be objective from behind your own eyes.

Some people think that pushing good things away means they are humble and that's good somehow. But it just diverts the river of good away from you and down to someone else.

Giving and receiving should be in a flow. If you're a great giver but not a great receiver, you're not going to be allowing the maximum, sustainable flow that you could otherwise. Think of a heartbeat and the flow. What happens if the heart only pushes out blood but doesn't receive it? Well, it would stop beating pretty quick. Or breathing...if you only exhaled, you wouldn't last long. Inhaling, receiving, it is a great thing. The deeper you exhale, the more you should inhale so that you can deeply exhale again. This may go against a lot of past programming but really start to notice where in your life you are blocking receiving good things and start to try to receive. It's probably going to feel awkward or uncomfortable at first like all new habits, but you will get used to it in time and it will feel so great.

Uncertainty

For some reason, we've tied certainty to security and that everything is OK. From habits and relationships, to expectations about life. We've then by default also tied uncertainty to the opposite of all those; insecurity and that everything is not OK.

Oopsie.

The truth is that every second of every day has nothing but uncertainty.

There are things that are higher or lower probability of happening, but nothing is set in stone until it has actually happened.

Remember Enron? From the outside and to a lot of investors, it looked like the most rock-solid investment a person could have. It seemed certain, or wise to put your life savings in there and be able to retire on them and relax. But it was just a hollowed out tower and one day it came crumbling down. This was to the shock and horror of thousands of investors. If they had banked on that investment being the only possible way they could survive in retirement, the realization of it was more than just losing all their money, it was losing their life, essentially – all they worked for up to that point and all they had or would have in the future. Horrific. When the stock market crashed in the past, a lot of people, older and younger too, chose to end their own lives because they viewed the loss of their money as the loss of their life already. But it's not. They had placed their certainty in something in the outer world instead of in themselves.

You've got to place your certainty in yourself; your talents, abilities, resourcefulness, and resilience. You've got to place your certainty in uncertainty –

that every moment of every day holds the potential for new things. This can be viewed as a tragedy (any moment, I could lose everything!) or a blessing (any moment, things could turn around for the better!).

To only trust that uncertainty means tragedy means to live in worry and anxiety all the time. To only trust that uncertainty means great things means to be blindsided and unequipped to deal with bad things that happen. And they do happen. To everyone. Even good people who do everything right.

To trust that anything can happen and in yourself means you will be able to discern and recognize bad things and handle them, and you will be able to recognize good things and welcome them into your life with appreciation and joy.

You get to choose. If you, like 99.9% of people have generations long habits of not realizing this, those old habits are going to take some time, awareness, and practice to develop into new, better habits. If you have chronic anxiety or any type of mental illness, the choices can be much more difficult and overwhelming than what a lot of other people feel. It's not easy.

But you still get to choose, every moment of every day, eventually turning those old habits into dust and the new habits into the way you automatically think.

What you choose is what you believe.

What you believe is what you look for and accept and receive into your reality when you find it.

"Placing it in God's hands," "Giving it up to God," "If it's meant to be, it's meant to be…", "Fate," or "Destiny."

These phrases are true when used in the correct way. They are not true when used incorrectly. Incorrect use is when someone is facing something overwhelming or a possible loss or break up, and they do absolutely nothing but use one of these phrases or words. Then when the bad thing happens or the good thing doesn't happen, they say, "it must not have been meant to be," or feel "God had other plans" for them or feel disappointed in God.

If you do nothing, nothing will happen.

The correct way of using them is doing your best, all that you can do out of faith, love, respect for the wishes of others, work, effort, and positive belief.

Then when your only option is to wait and see, these are perfect expressions. When it comes to success or health or even getting a job, you do all you can do to be the best version of you that you can be. If you are chosen or accepted, that is the place for you. If not, that isn't the place for you. In romantic relationships, respect for other people's wishes is the key. If you believe that person is the one and only one for you and pursue them relentlessly, that technically would be "doing all you can do," but it's not respecting their wishes. If they're not interested, they're not interested. You shouldn't want someone who isn't interested or someone who you feel you have to change for or try and prove yourself to be acceptable for anyway. Be your best and know what qualities you'd love in a person and if that one doesn't see it, that is truly not meant to be. But keeping your attention and efforts fixed on that person will prevent you from even being able to see the person who is exactly who you want without you having to convince them of a thing.

Losing Trust in Good Things and People

When you have dealt with disappointment, betrayal, tragedy, especially when you have been blindsided by them, you can lose trust in good things. Almost as if you're trying to prepare yourself for the other shoe to drop, to not get your hopes up that things can be great in your life. This is anxiety and feels like a growing tension, the longer and better things are. But it doesn't prepare you for the losses; it just robs you of the ability to enjoy the good times and your good fortune. It can lead to self-sabotage and looks on the outside to be an absence of gratitude. It's not so much an absence of gratitude due to actually being ungrateful, but for not allowing yourself to believe in and receive the good things. Anxiety is complex and can be a very difficult thing to heal from. It can help to consciously become grateful and pause for all of the good things in your life. All day every day. Engage your mind in being able to enjoy and feel joy for those things and people in those moments.

The truth is, you can trust that nothing lasts forever, that sometimes good things don't end well, and there are times you will get hurt.

That is part of life. But it's not all of life.

You can also trust that you will meet and love good people, have great times and amazing experiences in life, sometimes even just beautiful, tiny moments that you will remember for a lifetime.
Trust that, too.

ABOUT THE AUTHOR

Doe Zantamata was born and raised in Canada near Toronto. She attended university at Niagara University for two years before transferring to Florida State University and graduating with a BSc. in Biology. From there, she pursued many creative projects, including independent films, acting, and graphic design. She has been writing since the time she could hold a pen, but launched her social media pages in April 2011. The book series, "Happiness in Your Life," is a set of twelve short books, each on a specific aspect of life but all intertwined together in many ways.

Please visit:

www.HappinessInYourLife.com

and the blog:
www.theHiYL.com

Printed in Great Britain
by Amazon